Tennis Ace

Phil Kettle
illustrated by Craig Smith

Distributed in
the United States of America
by Pacific Learning
P.O. Box 2723
Huntington Beach, CA
92647-0723

Website:
www.pacificlearning.com

Published by Black Hills
(an imprint of Toocool Rules
Pty Ltd)
PO Box 2073
Fitzroy MDC VIC 3065
Australia
61+3+9419-9406

First published in the United States by Black Hills in 2004.
American editorial by Pacific Learning in 2004.
Text copyright © Phillip Kettle, 2001.
Illustration copyright © Toocool Rules Pty Limited, 2001.

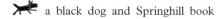 a black dog and Springhill book

Printed in China through Colorcraft Ltd, Hong Kong

ISBN 1 920924 04 3
PL-6205

10 9 8 7 6 5 4 3 2 1   08 07 06 05 04

Contents

Gemma Jones

Dog

Toocool

Chapter 1
Dueling Doubles

The voice on the loudspeaker was booming, "Ladies and gentlemen, welcome to the U.S. Open."

The crowd was clapping and cheering as we walked onto the tennis court.

"Ladies and gentlemen, please welcome the world's leading doubles team—Toocool and Gemma Jones."

We waved to the crowd. It felt great walking onto center court—even if I had to have Gemma for a partner. I wouldn't let her spoil this magnificent moment. I was a true professional.

I looked around the
stadium. The flowers were
perfect—except the ones Dog
was chewing.

The voice boomed again, "Now, please welcome two of the world's most promising players. Two players cemented together forever. Backyard's best doubles team—the amazing Brick and Wall."

Gemma and I looked at Brick and Wall. They were clearly a tough team. It would be challenging to get the ball past them.

Chapter 2
The Toocool Chant

Mom was in the backyard.

"Toocool, how many times have I told you not to wear your good clothes when you're playing outside?"

Mom never understood what was required when you were playing a professional sport.

"Toocool, go and get changed. While you're at it, make your bed!"

Being a sports professional was supposed to be fun. Why wasn't there someone to do my chores for me?

Gemma gave me a high five as I walked back to my locker room. Even she knew how I felt.

I checked out my old tennis whites in the mirror. They definitely needed help. I grabbed a marker. I wrote TOOCOOL CHAMPION across the back of the shirt.

Much better.

Then I looked in the locker-room mirror and asked, "Mirror, mirror on the wall, am I still the best of all?"

The mirror answered me, "Toocool, Toocool, you are best of all—until you take on Brick and Wall."

I tried not to think about what the mirror had said. My fans would be getting restless. Quickly, I checked the strings on my racket. They were tight enough to play music on. I had to get going.

As I jogged down the hall, I chanted to myself, "Toocool rules. Toocool rules."

I took a deep breath. I was ready to take on anyone. Even the awesome Brick and Wall.

Chapter 3
Tough Competition

The sun was shining on center court. The crowd was clapping and calling my name. I felt a shiver of excitement—the same one all great sports stars feel before a big game.

Everyone in the crowd was a blur, except for Bert the Rooster. He was sitting on top of the box seats. Dog was our ball boy. He stood on the sideline wagging his tail.

I did some stretches. I didn't want to strain any muscles. My fans needed me in top form.

I was ready to play.

We spun the racket, and I
won—as always. I decided to
serve first. I was serving to
Brick. I gave him the Toocool
glare. Brick glared back at me.
My first serve went straight
down the court.

Brick never moved, but he
hit the ball back at me. I hit a
forehand shot to Wall. Wall
played like Brick. She hit the
ball right back at me, too.

"Come on, Gemma. Take a shot," I yelled. She was grumpy. She had wanted to serve first.

I kept smashing the ball at Brick and Wall—backhand, forehand, straight down the line. I couldn't get the ball past them. For a moment I was worried. Maybe the mirror had been right.

Chapter 4
Toocool Is Hot

Then it happened. Deep from the back of the court, I hit the perfect lob. It shot straight over the top of Brick and Wall. They had no chance. It was way out of their reach. Toocool, Tennis Ace, had found Brick and Wall's weakness.

18

The crowd leaped up
together, clapping and cheering.
The ball fell off the garage
roof. Dog, the ball boy, brought
the ball back and dropped it at
my feet.

Now I was really firing. I served again. I glanced at the speed monitor. The serve was 150 miles per hour! The ball was moving so fast it was smoking!

Quick as a flash, Brick hit the smoking ball back at me. I thought it would go out, so I let it go.

The ball hit Dog right between the eyes. He looked dazed. Then he looked crabby. He bit the ball and wouldn't let go. We had to tackle him. Gemma held him down while I got the ball out of his mouth. It was all slimy and gross.

Next, I hit a spinning serve to Wall's backhand. The ball came back. I hit it down the middle. Brick smashed the ball back at me. I stretched as far as I could. Wham! I knocked it back. What a magical rally. Dog got dizzy trying to keep up.

Dog sprinted up and down the court. Being ball boy was exhausting him, but I just kept lobbing that ball. Even Gemma got in a few shots.

My final serve was sensational, but the ball didn't go where it was supposed to. It clipped Brick's edge, hit the court, and flew toward Mom's garden. Uh-oh.

Chapter 5

The Victory Dance

I dove for the ball. I swung my racket right through the flowerbed. Twenty daffodil heads went flying through the air, but I kept the ball in play. It was the winning shot! Game, set, and match to the great Toocool team.

I threw my racket in the air. I waved to the crowd. I leaped over the broken daffodils. I danced the Toocool victory dance.

A voice rang out from one of the box seats, "Toocool! What have you done to my garden? Look at my flowers! What were you thinking?"

I stopped dancing.

What? I thought. How could Mom be worried about a few flowers, when I had just won the U.S. Open?

Maybe she'll be nicer to me
when I'm a skateboard star.
The End!

Toocool's
Tennis Glossary

Backhand—A tennis shot made by reaching your racket arm across your body. (The back of your hand is facing the net.)

Forehand—A tennis shot made on the same side of your body as your racket arm. (The palm of your hand is facing the net.)

Lob—When you hit the ball high in the air and it lands on the other person's side of the court.

Rally—A rally is when the players hit the ball back and forth until a point is scored.

Toocool's Backyard
Tennis Court

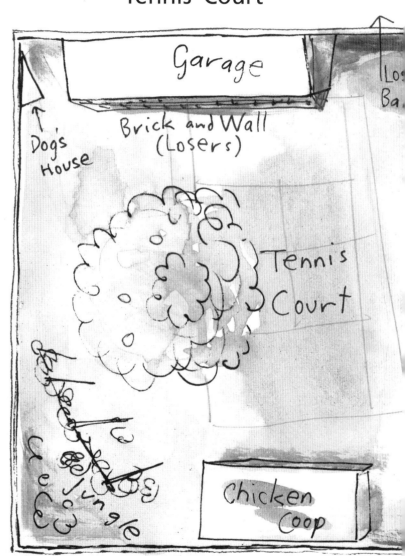

Garage

Brick and Wall
(Losers)

Dog's
House

Tennis
Court

Jungle

Chicken
Coop

Los...
Ba...

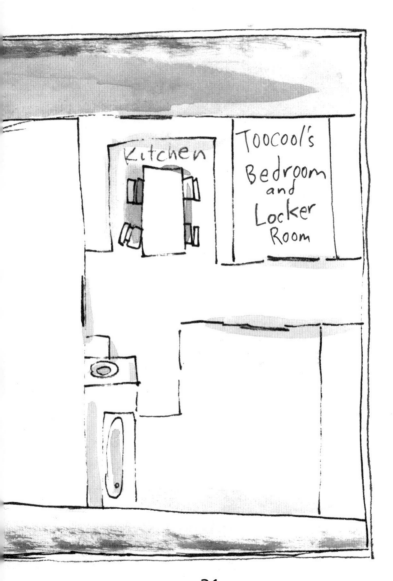

31

Toocool's Quick Summary
Tennis

Tennis is played in nearly all countries of the world. "Singles" is played by two people—one on each side of the court. "Doubles" is played by four people—two on each side of the court.

Tennis is played on surfaces like clay, grass, or special new stuff made just for sports surfaces. My own private tennis court is a little different. It's mostly grass, but it has a few clay spots, too.

A game of tennis is played by hitting the ball over the net and into the other side of the court. To win, you have to hit the ball so that the other player makes a mistake trying to hit it back to you.

The most famous tennis event is called the Grand Slam. There are four tournaments in the Grand Slam. They are the Australian Open, in Melbourne; the French Open, in Paris; Wimbledon, in London, England; and the U.S. Open, in New York.

One day, I plan to win all the tournaments in the Grand Slam.

The **Tennis** Court

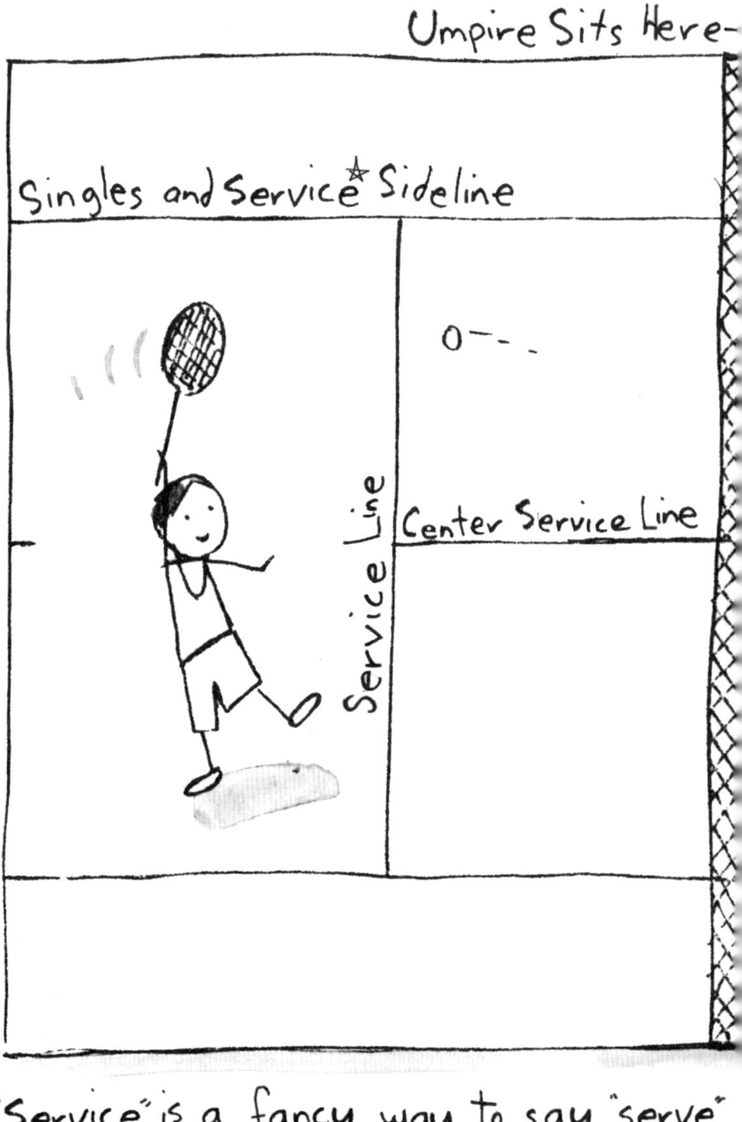

Umpire Sits Here—

Singles and Service* Sideline

Center Service Line

Service Line

* "Service" is a fancy way to say "serve".

Doubles Sideline

Baseline

←Net

Q & A with Toocool
He Answers His Own Questions

 **Toocool, what kind of surface do you like to play on?**

Well, I play a really fast game, so I prefer a hard surface. I've played on clay, but the clay slowed me down. I still won, but it slowed me down.

What's so special about your backyard court?

It has the best grass I've ever played on—especially when it's just been mowed. The other great thing is that I've got a brick wall instead of a net. Not many other courts have that. Playing against Brick and Wall has made me the champion I am today.

Do you have a good serve?

I have an incredible serve.
I think my serve is what scares other players the most. To stand before the Toocool serve is a very scary thing. I also have an amazing backhand. Other players always try to copy my forehand.

What is your greatest victory?

Winning the U.S. Open is my greatest victory. It was a fantastic way to end the year. Now that I've beaten Brick and Wall, I know I'll win the Grand Slam next year. That will be my next great victory—unless my opponents are too afraid to show up!

Who is the greatest player you have ever seen?

I'm the greatest player I have ever seen. Next to me, I think anyone in the top ten is pretty cool. They all watch my game closely. They like to be ready for new competition.

What advice would you give to people who are starting to play tennis?

I would tell them to find their own brick wall, even if it's in a park or at school. A brick wall has the fastest return you will ever play against. If you can beat a brick wall, you can beat anyone.

I would also tell them that it's *hot* out there. Wear lots of sunscreen. You don't want a sunburned nose when the photographers take your picture.

Tennis Quiz

How Much Do You Know about Tennis?

Q1. If you serve a fault, what have you done?

A. Hit the dog with the ball.
B. Hit the ball outside the court lines. **C.** Dropped a plate while doing the dishes.

Q2. If the score is deuce, what has happened?

A. You are winning. **B.** You are losing. **C.** The score is tied.

Q3. Which player has the best chance of winning the Grand Slam next year?

A. Brick. **B.** Wall. **C.** Toocool.

🎾 **Q4** What is a ball boy or girl?
A. Someone who sells tennis balls.
B. A person who bounces around like a ball. *C.* A person who collects the ball between points.

🎾 **Q5** Toocool serves an ace. What has he done?
A. Cooked a meal. *B.* Won a game of cards. *C.* Won a point with a great serve.

🎾 **Q6** How many players are on the court in a game of singles?
A. 6. *B.* 2. *C.* 1.

🎾 **Q7** How many players are on the court in a game of doubles?
A. 8. *B.* 6. *C.* 4.

Q8 If you hit a great smash, what have you done?

A. Recorded a hit song. *B.* Ridden your bike into a fence. *C.* Hit a high ball very well.

Q9 If the dog runs away with the ball, what do you do?

A. Yell very loudly. *B.* Get another ball from your tennis bag. *C.* Fire the dog as ball boy.

Q10 The score is love. What does that mean?

A. Toocool is winning—and loving it. *B.* The scores are equal. *C.* No one has scored.

ANSWERS

🎾 **1** B. 🎾 **2** C. 🎾 **3** C. 🎾 **4** C.
🎾 **5** C. 🎾 **6** B. 🎾 **7** C. 🎾 **8** C.
🎾 **9** B. 🎾 **10** C.

If you got ten questions right,
Toocool would like to meet you.
If you got between five and nine
questions right, you're not quite
ready for the Grand Slam. If you
got fewer than five right, you
might be a good ball kid.

TOO COOL

Skateboard Standout

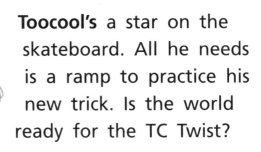

Toocool's a star on the skateboard. All he needs is a ramp to practice his new trick. Is the world ready for the TC Twist?

Titles in the Toocool series